T0198878

A Time For Marriage

A Married Couples Quick Go-to-Guide

SUSIE WRIGHT ENOCH

To order additional copies of this book, contact:
Xlibris
844-714-8691
www.Xlibris.com
Orders@Xlibris.com

Library of Congress Control Number: 2023904484
ISBN: Softcover   978-1-6698-7006-7
           Hardcover   978-1-6698-7005-0
           EBook   978-1-6698-7007-4

Print information available on the last page

Rev. date: 03/08/2023

References

Unless otherwise indicated, all scripture quotations were taken directly from the King James Bible. Any additional quotes used were provided below with the person's name given to credit. All photos and images used were through iStock and Getty Images.

Dedication

I wish to dedicate this book to my loving husband, Timothy,

who always cheers me on throughout life. It is my life with you that I've learned

how blessed it is to find that special person in one's life. I'm thankful we found

each other. The two shall be as one.

A Time for Marriage

A Married Couple's Guide

Contents

Introduction

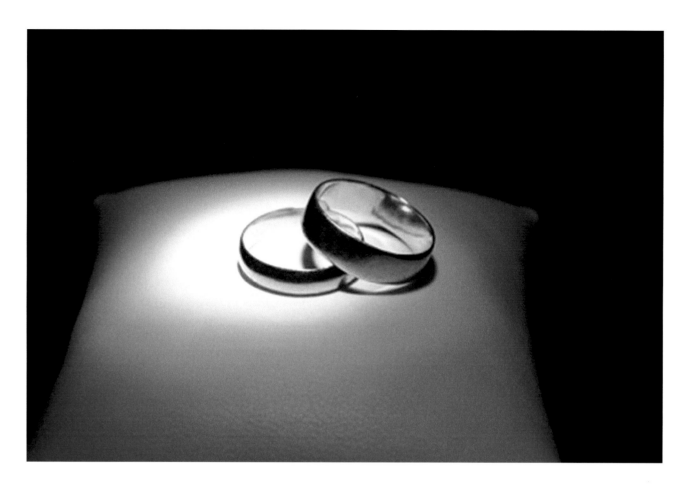

Marriage, like any other relationship, takes love, time, effort, and total commitment. It is indeed a sacred institution initiated, blessed, and protected by God Himself, who, with divine intentions, created marriage to be innocent, pure, and holy, blessed within the world he created solely to be loved, honored, worshipped, and obeyed by its inhabitants (Genesis 2:21–25). For God created and designed the union of marriage when the world was perfect, not perverted with human sins full of lustful desires, fornication, greed, or envy.

From the beginning, Satan set out to destroy this divine relationship for it was and remains important to God and signifies what our relationship is with him. Satan sets up a plan to (1) tempt Eve to rebel against God with twisted words, and (2) through her temptation and Adam's weakness to protect her, the door was opened to mankind's fall, succumbing to sin through willful disobedience (Genesis 3:1). Satan's attempts to hinder the marriage relationship are mainly to distort humanity's perception of love and holiness, ultimately causing us to live in a complete state of rebellion, being estranged and separated from God.

Today, when we view the statistics, divorce rates are staggering. Marriages start so promisingly, but a few years down the road, marriages fall apart. Why? Those in the marriage fail to maintain the most important factors in the relationship—love, time, and commitment. Unless we learn the basic functions of a relationship, we will continue to experience these issues at a higher rate.

First of all, we need to recognize people marry for the wrong reasons. Some marry for physical attraction. Some marry because of pressure from family and friends. Others just marry for no specific reason but to be married. For they love the idea of "belonging" to another in marriage. Sadly, these marriages are doomed before they can even begin. These individuals involved fail to understand that what brings them together can keep them together—at least most of the time. But unfortunately, life can change things. People gain weight for all kinds of reasons: medication, childbearing, age, or medical problems. Men or women may lose their hair due to illnesses, medication, and worries of life, and there is the dreaded knowledge we all change over time. All these things can cause stress in the best of relationships. It takes true love to overcome the problems in life that all couples face. It seems when we marry, many of us believe the romance stops, and so does the need for commitment to each other. A relationship is like a delicate flower. If you care for it, it will bloom year after year, yielding its luscious beauty for everyone to see. If you don't, you will probably end up with just a dried-up stem, lifeless and with no desire to survive withering from the inside out.

So let us now take a closer look at some of the situations couples need to address before and after marriage. I guarantee you and many others will find a little of yourselves somewhere within the pages of this book. Don't worry, no one will ever know but you, unless you willingly desire to divulge that secret. Just showing a little humor here, for marriage, after all, is serious. In the following chapters, just take note and evaluate where you and the one you love are in your relationship. Everyone needs to take a consistent thirty-day evaluation in life. This enables one to stay aware of the little things that creep up in our relationships that may fester into major situations. Let's begin!

Chapter 1

Is He or She the One?

As you know, every relationship starts hot and heavy—even more, you can't seem to keep your hands off each other. But if it is a meaningful relationship, you are seeking more. You know it's not just about being sexually compatible. If it's to be meaningful, the physical attraction will be there, but it's not what is going to keep you in the relationship. Every relationship goes through developmental stages when it comes to intimacy. In the beginning, you can't think of anything else. You daydream constantly when you are apart. You often find yourself reminiscing about your shared moments, how they looked the last time you saw them, or the pure joy of their touch. Either way, the relationship will change. The lust-filled stage will become the companion stage.

If this is depressing to you, it should not be. After all, no relationship should base itself merely on sex. Relationships are built on companionship. From birth, every one of us is bound to be in a relationship. From the love of our parents to childhood friends to our first love, we are framed by the memories of deep, meaningful relationships.

These relationships are bound by what we know of the person's likes and dislikes. It is the things we share emotionally and physically that bring us closer to connecting with others—the things that make us feel good and feel comfortable enough to share our lives with them. These are the same connections we must take in our permanent relationships such as marriage. Individuals must take the time to be confident when it comes to a lasting commitment to another person.

How do you do this? By asking questions and getting to know them other than being sexually intimate. When the hard times come in a relationship, you can't be a mind reader if your better half will endure the test. You need to know the mind and heart of a person. A person's background can give you clues into how they have moved around in the world before you.

Below are some relevant questions to ask yourself before entering into a relationship that includes a life commitment.

1. What are you looking to get from the person?

Attraction is important and so is the ability to traverse the changes that will occur over one's lifetime. How will you feel twenty or thirty years from now if everything is determined by pure attraction? Remember, life has a way of causing people to undergo significant changes, both mentally and physically. Ladies, do you know that most men deal with drastic hair loss at a certain age? They go bald. According to the National Library of Medicine, male pattern baldness affects 82 percent of men by the age of eighty[1]. The full head of hair he possesses now may change a few years down the road. And those rippling abs and powerful muscles you see in the early stages may change to a not-so-toned and muscular physique. And men, please understand most women gain weight due to stress, childbearing, and menopause issues. Remember, life changes us mentally, emotionally, physically, and spiritually. Can you still love each other if and when such changes occur?

2. Are you compatible? Do you share core values?

If you only believe sharing a sexual relationship with a person determines if one is marriage material, think again. Sex is not enough to build a meaningful and lasting relationship for life. Find out who the person is as an individual. Have meaningful conversations with each other. Ask relevant questions that will enable you to see their character and their heart. Do you enjoy the same foods? What are your thoughts about relationships and intimacy? What are your interests? What are their aspirations in life?

What do love and family look like to them? What are their religious beliefs? What do they believe about premarital sex? These are just some of the questions you need to know firsthand to weed out potential threats to the kind of meaningful relationship you are seeking to have with another person.

If they are topping the charts of a "winner," ask yourself how comfortable you are with this person. How would your life look like with this person on a day-to-day basis? Can you truly open your heart to this person, share the most intimate and deepest part of your life with them, and feel secure doing it? If for any reason you feel hesitant to discuss your life and past experiences, I urge you right now to reevaluate your relationship at this point. Often, being hesitant is a warning sign that either you are not ready to make a permanent commitment, or they may not be the one for you. If they are the right person, the ability to share will come naturally.

To determine if the person you are involved with is the right one, you must gather the knowledge you need to make a proper conclusion. Remember, intimacy is good, but so is finding that special someone who will fulfill your life even more. You want to have someone who will go to war for you if need be—one who will pray for and with you, console you, love you, hold you, and cheer you on in good times and in bad. Make sure your core values are the same. Being unequally yoked will only bring more chaos and unhappiness in your marriage and your life.

Chapter 2

Time to Prepare for Your Marriage

Every year, my husband and I celebrate another wedding anniversary. I can't help but reflect on our past and the difference it has made in our lives to follow the path God had for us. When we reflect on the many years gone by, it is true to say that we are and have been very happy and in love. I must admit, those dating years were hard to navigate, and when it comes to marriage, it is even harder. Here are a few steps to help prepare you on your journey for your marriage:

1. **Pray.** Indeed, this is a crucial part of the preparation for married life and those preparing for marriage. It is equally important that family and friends pray with you and for you during this time. In your prayer time, be honest with God; humbly seek clarity about the one intended to be your future husband or wife. You must believe that God desires the best mate for you, someone who is loving, gentle, kind, caring, and considerate. Pray for wisdom and discernment that your heart,

as well as your eyes, be opened to what God needs you to see about the person you are praying for. Make sure you keep an open mind and heart. Listen intently and discern what the Spirit of the Lord is saying. Many times when God says "no," we ignore the warning. However, if God says "yes," then ask God to help mold and shape you for your future husband or wife. Praying is something you should have been doing all along in this area. Either way, be prepared to accept what He says and take heed.

2. **Stop having premarital sex**. If you are currently in a sexual relationship and are preparing to get married, stop and wait until you are man and wife. If your intended mate leaves you because of this, then you will know without a doubt that this person was not "the one" after all. It doesn't matter if you have a child with this person or if you have been newly dating or dating for one year or many years. A sexual relationship outside of marriage eats away at the moral fabric of the soul, dirties your self-respect, and separates you from the relationship you were meant to have with God. If you are a woman of great worth, then this type of relationship should be insulting to you. God never intended for you to be devalued by any man. If you are a man, and the woman has initiated this type of relationship, you should be equally concerned. Men, a woman should never offer you her body as a sample item to taste before marriage. Let me say this: By not waiting, you are the one in control of your life, and you are choosing your own path. When you choose your own path over the one God has for you, you are missing the opportunities to meet and be with your true soulmate.

3. **Spend alone time with God and His word.** If you feel your worth is defined by having a man in your life and having that man stay in your life depends on you giving him your precious body, then you need to spend much more alone time with God and His word. Men, you are susceptible to these lies as well. Satan will have you thinking that ALL women want to be sexually active with a man to love him, respect him, and honor him. Understand that these are Satan's lies. Understand that this is NOT the intimacy and connection either of you desires. Satan tells us fulfillment is readily available to us through sex. This is a huge lie designed to make us think less of ourselves and destroy our self-worth. This type of behavior separates us from God.

4. **Get yourself and your prospective mate healthy—emotionally, spiritually, and physically.** Join a church where the two of you can worship as a couple. A couple needs to worship together and build a true foundation for their family. Share the unity of love that you have been blessed with by helping others and getting involved.

5. **Be patient.** While it may feel that God is making you both wait forever, He is still preparing you for an ordained connection. Remember, He could still be at work in your future mate too. Even though you may be ready in God's eyes, your soulmate may not fully be ready. Be still while He readies him or her for you. Be patient, be loving, and have faith. God is working it all out for both of you!

Chapter 3

The Ceremony: Is It Meaningful or Is It for Show?

If we take a closer look at the traditional marriage ceremony, we find it full of action verbs stating promises to love, cherish, honor, nurture, support, take care of, and grow with. We all know the word *action* means or suggests "an ongoing active pursuit of a goal." Nowhere do the vows say, "I promise to love, honor, and care for you only when time permits." But vows of marriage are to be words that are full of promise, and everyone knows it takes time for promises to be taken seriously.

Instead of creating precious moments with our spouse that will solidify the commitment between us, we place our focus on the ceremony. Many of us take months and perhaps one or two years to plan our wedding day. We bombard our minds with decisions regarding cake samples and rummage through photos of flower arrangements and other wedding decorations. We focus our sights on the attire for the bride and the groom, the wedding party, wedding venues, and so on. We take more time in preparing for this day to show off for friends and family than we do to sit down and talk about the expectations we have for the marriage.

Yet today, marriage in America is on its way out. We seem to care so much about other things such as culture, fashion, TV, sports, and careers that our relationships suffer. Countless women have confided to me that when their spouses come to bed, so do the ESPN commentators. These women are starving for attention, companionship, love, time, and intimacy with their spouses. The husbands complain that their wives are "naggers." From the time they enter the home, the chatter never stops. One husband shared with me that as soon as he comes home, his wife stands at the door and follows him around the house, complaining about her day. Other husbands complain that the house is never clean. The mother-in-law, sister, or girlfriends are always present, and there never seems to be any private time to wind down from a hectic day. Husbands complain that their wives are always busy helping the kids and then come to bed with rollers in their hair and beauty cream or mud masks on their faces, ready to snuggle. Their wives consistently sleep in faded T-shirts and raggedy gowns with stains and walk around in big fuzzy slippers and complain of intimacy. One husband during a consultation became so frustrated in describing his spouse's nightwear that he completely ripped the buttons off his shirt. Little to say, his wife was horrified at the intensity of his displeasure.

The marriage ceremony is to be meaningful, not entertaining. You are not actors putting on a theatrical performance for critical reviews. Make your wedding day special, but keep it God-centered and sacred. After all, it is ordained and instituted by God to be carried out through commitment and love between a man and a woman. One thing you ladies may find interesting in particular is that from my conversations with males who are married, they felt they had no "say-so" in the planning of their weddings with their bride-to-be. Many of the men still harbor ill feelings with their spouses over the issues, and all I can say is, "Ladies, please allow your man to have input into the planning." It's his special day too! True, most men do not fantasize about a wedding day, but when it is evident the day is coming, they want input too!

Let the ceremony be about the two of you and God. Whether you decide on a small intimate wedding or an all-blow-out one with two hundred guests or more, that's your thing. Just remember, it's not about materialism or price. It will eventually be about the two of you in the long run. Don't let all the opinions of others infiltrate what is to be a special time for the two of you. After all, your mate and the life you two are preparing together should be the focus. No one else's needs or opinions should apply. If your family members love and value your union, they will be excited and happy to simply be a part of your special day. The rest is just secondary.

Chapter 4

"I, _____, take thee, _____, to be my wedded wife/husband,
to have and to hold from this day forward, for better, for worse,
for richer, for poorer, in sickness and in health, to love and to
cherish, till death do us part, according to God's holy ordinance.
And thereto I pledge thee my faith."

The Vows

The most important moment of the wedding ceremony is the exchanging of **vows**. What do these vows mean? Well, they appear to be simple little words, but in reality, they are a powerful and binding force between you and the person you are joining with before a Holy God. They are the words that will bind you in love and life "through sickness, and health, and for richer or for poorer." There will be times down through the years when they will come back to you time and time again. There will be moments you will ask yourselves, did we honor them? Do they bear any resemblance to what was felt when the two of you gazed into each other's eyes and spoke so passionately? Time will tell the story!

Everyone wants their wedding vows to be beautiful and meaningful. The wedding vows are meant to show how generous our love will be. They are meant to show how patient, kind, and caring we promise to be with our mates. Yet there are hidden vows we are also making, whether we wish to admit it or not. These are as follows:

1. **The vow to enter a long-term relationship (preferably forever)**. A relationship of committed love, united in terms of home and family. A vow that promises stability but can never truly offer it due to life and its ever-changing winds and seasons. Marriage is like the weather. You wake up together every morning but never really know what the temperature or climate will be throughout the day. For the most part, it will be sunny and warm, and you will bask in those days and kiss the sweet wind when it blows across your face. Then there will be days when you will experience the arctic cold and harsh strong winds. These are the days when you will need to bundle up, hold on, and snuggle closer together. Just remember that marriage is about sharing your life with one person for the rest of your life, building on the love you share, and learning to fall even deeper in love as time moves on. If you can't make this commitment, don't get married until you can. It will serve you both better in the long run. Remember, it's a sacred institution.

2. **The vow to love when your other half irritates you.** This will happen more often than you realize. You are learning to be a couple; there is nothing temporary to marriage. It's binding and real. Listen, as a new couple, you are learning to share your life with another person. Sharing brings on some issues. For example, you are a perfectionist; your partner is not. You want ten kids; your partner prefers two. You like things in their proper place; your partner puts things wherever they feel it's convenient. You are a saver; your partner loves to spend. You like meat; your partner is a vegetarian. You want a walk-in ready home; they want a fixer-upper. These are issues that should be discussed and settled before marriage, but if not, they are things you will mostly have to learn to live with. Compromise on those irritating things. Some can be a little comical; some not. But this is normal, and in time, with much love and many deep breaths, you will survive. Some habits can be overlooked. However, some cannot. Things like gambling, overspending, and going out with friends regularly can lead to major problems. Know your mates' habits, likes, and dislikes.

3. **The vow to love even when you are unhappy**. Every couple goes through these times. No one person can make someone happy. Happiness comes from within. If you are happy with your life, it will show in what you do for each other. It will allow you both to grow and spread outward. You will desire to be more than you are. You will embrace life with a fuller capacity to live it more productively. But there will be times when you will be unhappy. Life is full of surprises, and one thing is for sure: We all get there at one time or another. We can't be happy 24/7. It's not natural, but just pray about what it is you are unhappy about. There are times we misconstrue what is happening around us or what the other person is going through. Take time to evaluate what makes you happy and what happiness looks like to you.

4. **The vow to love even when the relationship has been compromised**. Love is complicated. Relationships can be complicated. Marriage is very complicated. When we take the vow "to love, honor, and obey," we must be REAL. It's deep. No one can predict the future. No one can tame the heart. Situations happen to the best of marriages, but one thing is for sure: If the love in the marriage is real, it can survive. I have had to counsel many couples where infidelity was their number one issue. I did find out that most times, the person who committed the trespass was attempting to relive an issue they never had the opportunity to get closure on. Exes have a way of entering our lives at a point of unhappiness in our present relationships. Just know it is best to never go back to anything you had to pray your way out of! If it was toxic in the past, it will be toxic in the present and so in the future.

Chapter 5

Time for Commitment = Prayer & Intimacy

Have you ever wondered why once we begin dating, our thoughts become cluttered and centered on being with the one "we" love? We all have jobs or are in school during this time, yet we find time to date. My father would say to couples he counseled in marriage, "Whatever you do in the courting relationship is what you will have to continue doing throughout the marriage." It is our idea of love that brings on thoughts of intimacy with someone. All couples experience this emotional roller coaster, and they all get sick once it starts to slow down. However, nothing can be more delusional than to think we can marry and live happily ever after without committing time toward its success.

Any businessperson can tell you that success comes with work and that time is the key element to success. Besides, we go to college to enhance our knowledge and understanding of our talents and skills in hopes of being successful. So why should we believe or think that marriage is not worth the same thought? Is anything in life worth having without time and sacrifice? The only way a marriage can truly be successful is by keeping it together through time, intimacy, and prayer. The Apostle Paul speaks about marriage in I Corinthians 7:3–5. It says,

"Let the husband render to his wife the affection due her, and likewise also the wife to her husband. The wife does not have authority over her own body, but the husband does. And likewise, the husband does not have authority over his own body, but the wife does. Do not deprive one another except with consent for a time that you may give yourselves to fasting and prayer; and come together again so that Satan does not tempt you because of your lack of self-control."

It doesn't take a rocket scientist to interpret this passage. It simply means the marriage vows spoken include responsibilities for both partners. Here, the scripture tells us that we are one flesh and that we belong to each other. We are not to deprive or withhold ourselves from intimacy with each other unless it is in time before God through prayer and fasting. If a bachelor such as Paul could understand the importance of commitment, what's our excuse? God instituted distinct instructions for a successful union of marriage. Why? God values unity and places high standards of importance when it comes to the well-being of the man and woman's relationship. He desires the marriage union to be a commitment between two people: bearing the seal of being sacred and holy before Him. Whenever in doubt, the Word of God will enlighten us as our guide for life.

Yet the word "commitment" brings fear in many relationships. Many vow to be joined and connected with their partners, often moving in together but never fully committing to the marriage. They go through the actions of commitment but fail to understand one never enters a *true* relationship without reciprocity. You can never get back what you do not give in the relationship. Marriage requires one to be self-sacrificing and compromising. Without commitment, one is never married in heart, for it only leads to infidelity. For as soon as the first little test comes and the winds begin to blow, the couple becomes weak and frustrated, and someone, if not both, walks away from the relationship.

Commitment is another word for "promise, pledge, and vow." All relationships are tested for us to know the depth of our loyalty to them. Despite the fact marriage is ordained by God, it will be tested. Remember, our commitment solidifies the love within our relationships. Though the winds may rise, do not run. Fall on your knees, pray together, and allow your marriage to be lifted before God and blessed.

Chapter 6

Time for Silence?

Now let's discuss the old cliché that says, "Silence is golden." In many situations, silence is "golden," but in marriage, it is often not. Silence creates distance, separation, and mistrust, and it dries up the passion or romance between a man and a woman like weeds in the desert. Never allow the tumbling tumbleweeds to stop at your door of love.

Many times, when there are problems in marriages, we hoard our feelings inside and allow them to go on for years. The more time we allow issues to go unresolved the greater the issues become. They fester and germinate inside, and even the smallest incident or misunderstanding is now an all-out war zone.

But in marriage, silence is often used when we do not have the ability to communicate effectively with the other person. An example would be men tend to shut down when women want to talk—especially when it comes to love and the need for it. This lack of communication causes a warped feeling inside the core of the relationship, prompting the women to initiate a confrontation. However, men display a **code of silence** when they are guilty as charged. My advice here is to keep this one thing in the forefront of your mind: When couples fail to communicate with each other, the spirit of "breakup" steps forward, all the while anticipating the arrival of its *old* friend "divorce" to take over and destroy what could easily have been a "happily ever after."

Remember: It is always best to talk out one's differences and all misunderstandings in a relationship—especially in marriage before newer and bigger problems take center stage.

There are at least **four** major issues all marriages face at one time or another. If you are experiencing one of these, just sit down and discuss them calmly.

1. **Money Problems.** It is the number one problem or issue couples face. He wants a new car, and she wants to do renovations on the house. He wants to pay the bills, but she spent the money on a new living room set. She wants to expand the business, but he wants a motorcycle to feel the wind in his face. Priorities in the household must be dealt with first before personal desires can be met. Compromise as to when certain things like a new dress or new electronic gadgets can be purchased without putting the family in a bind. Sit down as a couple, adopt a budget plan, and stick to it. Keep a "rainy-day" fund for emergencies. Couples need to pool their funds together until the household finances improve enough to the point they can go with separate accounts later.

2. **Relatives and Friends.** This is the second most confrontational issue among couples. Never allow your family and friends to dictate the dos and don'ts in your relationship. Never have Mom and Dad over every night for dinner or to just sit around every day. **Besides, this usually happens when one spouse remains dependent on his or her parents for emotional and financial support.** Ladies, please be careful of this if you have a very independent man at home. Never say to your husband, "Well, Daddy brought mother one when they were first married." And men, please do not compare your wife's cooking or her housekeeping skills to your mother's. No wife wants to be told, "Honey these biscuits are not like my momma's biscuits."

   The same applies to your siblings. Sisters and brothers should not have a key to your home and come in when they feel the urge. It should only be for emergencies and not when they want a place to hang out.

As for friends, Bob, Sally, Ted, and Alice need to stay at their house sometimes, keep their advice and opinions to themselves, and let the two of you live your life. Too many people and too many influences can spoil the moment. Share your precious time together in moderation. No one likes an audience all the time. Not even actors.

3. **Intimacy.** All marriages experience problems in this area at one time or another. Marriage is a beautiful institution, but there is more to a relationship than the physical benefits. Get focused and realize that life changes things. Marriage involves having children, working several jobs, and eventually, health issues can cut down your time together dramatically. Find time to go on intimate rendezvous together and just learn to be together. Wake up early in the morning to make your spouse a cup of tea or coffee, go out on the veranda, and share with each other the peace and tranquility of your surroundings before starting your day. A quiet moment together allows us to feel an even closer expression of intimacy, especially when we can share a touch of the hand, a special look, wink, or smile with the one we love. Taking time to place a love note in your spouse's briefcase or jacket pocket can brighten and deepen those moments of love you share. It's truly the simple things in life we cherish and remember the most. However, being intimate with each other does not always mean one has to be sexually intimate but the ability to touch another person's heart—that is an art. Learn to be artistic!

4. **Partner Expectations.** *This is a real issue.* Exactly who does what in the marriage? This should have been decided long before walking down the aisle. Men, you must not assume the little woman is going to be in the role of the "happy housewife." Women, we must not assume that because we both work, hubby is going to do half of the housework. Never assume the roles in marriage automatically happen the way we are familiar with thinking or seeing. Again, all issues need to be discussed and agreed upon before marriage. Take time to know how you fit in each other's life.

These four things, minor as they seem, are the most confrontational issues couples deal with in marriage. Yes, silence is golden in some instances. But don't use it as a weapon to hurt or ignore vital issues that need to be resolved. Learn to talk things out and then learn to let them go when there is no resolution. Continue to love each other enough to admit when the problem is greater than the two of you.

Under no circumstances whatsoever let yourself at any time verbally and physically abuse or threaten your spouse. **What is abuse or a threat?** It is a gesture or an act that is designed to create physical or emotional pain in your partner. If the relationship between the two of you is becoming more aggressive by means of shouting, screaming, throwing objects, and getting physical. **Be quiet!** In this instance, "**silence is golden**," so is leaving until the atmosphere is more presentable. If this type of situation happens, I would thoroughly and carefully suggest some form of professional counseling for you both.

Chapter 7

Time for You, Me . . . Kids?

Marriage is great, and all its perks are even more exciting. But what about the kids? Oh no, did we not discuss children? Many times, when people date and decide to marry, they omit or forget in the hustle and bustle of dating the little fact that . . . intimacy brings on babies. Perhaps you are one of those individuals who never see themselves as someone's parent. Having children is normal in marriage, and I am hoping that it will be a major discussion before the relationship gets too serious . . . like marriage.

But don't take it for granted that your partner is enthusiastic about it. Ladies, do not assume your husband wants to be a father six months into the marriage, especially if he has high hopes of becoming another Wall Street tycoon. This advice also applies to men. Never assume the little woman desires to be the mother of your children. Women today are equally minded when it comes to having their own money and careers.

However, there are times when it is not about the money or their careers but the fear that the intimacy of the relationship would change once a child comes into the fold. True, their relationship will change. Fear of losing quality time with someone you love can be terrifying and overwhelming. The idyllic moments of being spontaneous and sharing carefree and intimate moments with each other will be over. A child changes the entire trajectory of a relationship. They will need constant supervision, care, and love. Many begin to feel when a child enters the relationship all the love and romance once shared with their significant other flies out the window.

But don't fret. A child can bring deeper love to the relationship. A child teaches one responsibility, and it allows you to develop other ways to share the love you have with your mate. A child is a beautiful blend of your love—the love you share together.

Unfortunately, many marriages have ended in divorce when pregnancies happen, especially unwanted pregnancies. If the marriage relationship happens to be on shaky ground, never assume an innocent child will be welcomed. Most often, an unwanted pregnancy will only add to the stress of the situations going on in the marriage, and resentment can build up quickly toward the child. This is a subject that must be discussed openly and honestly beforehand.

Children are a blessing, but an unwanted pregnancy before or during marriage can cause resentment for both partners. Unwanted pregnancies can cause an individual to feel trapped. Never attempt to force a pregnancy on your mate, thinking they will change their minds once the baby comes. It could backfire. Being dishonest in your marriage at any time can bring on unwanted repercussions. If you are both not ready to become parents, then discuss your feelings, your thoughts, and the methods of contraception necessary to prevent an unwanted pregnancy until the desired time in your marriage. A child should be born into an atmosphere of love and expectancy from both his or her parents. Let it be a joyous time!

If you both are of different backgrounds racially, ethnically, or religiously, then it is pertinent you come to a decision or agreement as to which culture and religion (*if any*) the child will be brought up under. The Bible distinctly says, "Train **up a child in the way** he should go: and when he is old, he will not depart from it" (Proverbs 22:6).

Chapter 8

Time to Nurture

Intimacy is the next issue we must address. Emotional intimacy is vital in a marriage because it allows couples the opportunity to connect with each other. Intimacy needs the pleasure of touching, connecting, and embracing, and as humans, we long for its depths. Even though intimacy is something we all feel we know about, it seems to be one of the biggest problems most couples face in marriage.

There is a nurturing process for intimacy; it must be respected, honored, and reverenced. Marriage is a sacred union, and this means it is "precious." No, it is not a baby, but intimacy needs to be fed. When we commit ourselves to the unity of marriage, we are promising that we will meet the emotional and physical needs of the other. It is an effortless gift of oneself to another.

Nurturing is a sensitive process. Look at a flower; it needs water and sunlight to survive. Without these two main components, the flower loses its splendor and beauty. It becomes brittle and dry, eventually falls into pieces, and is blown away. This is what happens in marriage if intimacy is not nurtured. The intimacy dries up and causes the couple to experience an outburst of anger, resentment, bitterness, and rigidity, and it loses its luster and elasticity to snap back after conflict. Eventually, the relationship dies. But if it is nurtured tenderly with water, proper sunlight, and a little extra loving care, it thrives and lives beyond its natural cycle.

So what is nurturing? It is the skill to place an affirmation of love into another person's heart and life. It tells the other person your level of commitment to the relationship, allowing the outpouring of submissiveness of your heart to the one you love in a confirmation of "yes." This allows you to give yourself unconditionally, that you are willing to let yourself love and be loved.

Nurturing is learning to touch the heart of the person you are connected to. It is the union of caressing, touching, and finding a secure place in each other. Learn to know about each other rather than being all physical. If a marriage is based upon the sexual aspects of the relationship, it will fail. That person whom you have decided to share your life with is so much more than a body. They consist of feelings, dreams, and emotions. The need to belong to someone "special" is everyone's dream. I do not mean in the sense of becoming a piece of *property* but having that special person to share ourselves with.

Ladies, there are a couple of things we need to consider. One is that for men, intimacy is sometimes hard for them to cope with. It is up to you to show your mate that you will be patient in dealing with his feelings. Besides, men love being with a woman who makes them feel like a man. That is respecting him and taking time to show what you want from him in a relationship. Men want their relationships to be successful just like their careers. To a man, failure is death. Learn to listen and be there emotionally for them. Sometimes, that is all any of us really need. Men appreciate your presence more than your conversation.

A second thing to know is that women are more complex than men. We are emotional and intelligent creatures. We observe everything. If our mate is unhappy, we will know it. But sometimes, we are so observant that we take on the burden of insecurity, thinking it is something we are doing or that he is not happy in the relationship. Half the time, it is not even about us but something they are just dealing with. It could be job pressures, insecurity in them, fear of failing, fear of not providing sufficiently for the household, and many other things.

Men, it's your turn to get a few pointers. We must let you in on a secret or two about us. We want to be caressed, loved, respected, and cherished. There it is in a nutshell.

What is so hard about that? It is a simple description of what we WOMEN are . . . the beautiful precious creatures God created us to be . . . To YOU!

So let's get down to business. First, ladies like surprises, and most of all, we like romance. Sure, we know for a fact that there are no Prince Charmings. We just like to think there is. We want our mates to be a friend, a confidante, a lover, a teacher, a provider, a protector, and a father figure to our children. If you can master all these, you are good to go. But all jokes aside, women want godly men. If you are a man who loves and knows the Lord above all else, you are **the Man**. A godly man is one who has all the attributes described along with a "praying man." Nothing is more beautiful to us than a man who knows how to pray and lead the family into prayer when times permit. A man who will intercede for his family is what it's all about. A man who has so much love he is willing to go and call on heaven for his family. A "godly" man is the type of man that women don't mind walking beside or showing respect to. If you know the love of God and have a personal relationship with him, you will know how to love your wife.

Nurturing involves taking the time to learning what is important to you and your spouse. Being physically and sexually intimate is a beautiful thing between a man and a woman, but having **emotional intimacy** is more precious than gold in a marriage. In emotional intimacy, you will know the real person, what their heart's desire is, and the inner part of that person. It is the essence of the soul we need to handle with utter tenderness.

Remember, God wants us to have the fullness of love, intimacy, and purpose in life. He ordained marriage as *good*. Let us bring the will of God and His purpose for our lives back to the garden. **Take the time to know and really love each other.**

Chapter 9

Time to Maintain a Successful Marriage

These eight simple steps are just a few to keep handy and recall when you start to feel alone, unwanted, and unfulfilled in your relationship. Remember, keep God first in your relationship and, if in doubt, go before him for guidance. He is the best teacher after all.

1. **Make time for your relationship.** Take a day and set aside for the two of you to spend time together. Let everyone know that this is your special time to keep. This will give you both something to look forward to during your hectic work schedules. Meet somewhere special after work, perhaps at a restaurant or the movie theater. Go to Bible class and prayer meetings together. (This is the most opportune time to make God first in your relationship.)
2. **Communicate with each other.** Write small notes and place them in his/her lunch bag, briefcase, or coat pocket. If he/she goes to the gym after work, place

a love note in their gym shoes or gym shorts (have fun with this). Call each other at work just to say, "I love you." **(Verbal statements affirming love bring a great deal of emotional security to many of us.)** In the morning, give each other a goodbye kiss and a tender embrace and vice versa when coming home. Set aside time to listen when he/she wants to talk about work. Listening is the key to good communication. Don't ignore your mate and stick your fingers in your ears if it goes on over five minutes. If possible, turn the TV off, send the kids to their rooms, and give your mate your undivided attention. Never assume that your spouse can read your mind.

3. **Resolve family conflicts quickly.** Never go to bed with a bad taste in your mouth. Never allow family issues to go unresolved, not even for a few hours. Remember that communication is the key. If your silence could remedy the situation, then keep quiet. Remember, **silence is golden**.

4. **Make romance an everyday thing.** Ladies, this is so simple. Wake your husband on the weekends with a cup of coffee and a kiss. Prepare breakfast early one morning and serve it to him in bed before he dresses to go to work. Cook his favorite dish when he least expects it. Wear something other than that old Mickey Mouse nightgown you've had since high school. Invest in some nice lingerie; after all, he married you, not a bag lady. If you are planning on going out of town, then wear something that tantalizes him. I am not suggesting something too provocative, but find clothing that is tasteful and alluring at the same time. Ladies, keeping up your appearance is very important. No one is asking you to wear makeup 24/7, but men like to know you want to look your best for them. Remember, no one wants a person no one else finds attractive. We should never become too complacent about our looks and relationship and take them for granted. Ladies, you don't have to be a queen to look like one. This is one area that men consistently talk about that the wife seems to overlook.

Husbands, we don't want to leave you out. This same scenario given to the women can apply to you as well. Take the time to clean up properly. Ladies love their men to look nice and smell nice from time to time. Please take the time to put on nice shoes and leave the sneakers behind. Try wearing something dashing for a change when going out for dinner. Nothing exasperates a woman more than going out all dolled up and her man in tow with faded-out jeans, sneakers, and a comfy old sweater or faded shirt. Oh, and for goodness's sake, leave the baseball caps at home. Never sit at the table with your hat on. That is seen to be disrespectful of all women around you. Lastly, women want their men to treat them like royalty. In other words, they like to be courted. It's just that simple.

5. **Be respectful to your mate.** This is so important in marriage. Never talk about your intimate personal relationship with family or friends. Never speak ill of your spouse. When you do this, you're doing it to yourself. Remember you have become one flesh (Ephesians 5:31; Mark 10:8). Never belittle your mate to anyone. If there is something to be said, then always state the wonderful attributes that you admire. Always say, "Thank you" when your mate does something kind for you, no matter how small. (Always remember if you want respect, then give respect). Women, let's always be a Proverbs 31 woman. Men, remember that we are rare "jewels," not your doormats! Respect and protect!

6. **Give your spouse gifts.** Ladies, instead of buying yourself a new dress each payday, buy your hubby a shirt and tie set, his favorite cologne, or some aftershave. Show your love by treating him to a day at the spa for a manicure and pedicure. Men like to be pampered too! **Besides, it will keep his scratchy feet from cutting up your new bed sheets.** Just treat him the way you want to be treated. Men, the same rules apply. Don't go for broke on buying that new seventy-two-inch HD TV or new car stereo system. Remember the little woman at home. On your way home from work, stop and order some flowers and candies or take the time to run by her favorite store and buy her a nice fragrance from a nice department store. You know, something pretty for the both of you to enjoy from Victoria's Secret.

7. **Time for Intimacy.** God loves intimacy. Take time to worship together, pray together, and then separately. We must have a personal relationship with God, as well as with our spouse. Pray for God to continue to make you the husband and wife He desires for you to be . . . to help you learn submissiveness in your marriage to each other. Learning to have an intimate relationship with God will show you how to be intimate in your relationship.

8. **Know yourself.** Know who you are in Christ. To love someone else, we must first love ourselves. If facing the one in the mirror is a problem for you, then you have some issues that you personally need to address. Never enter a new relationship with emotional baggage from an old one. We must learn to evaluate ourselves and compare what we know to Christ. If it is not like him, then we need to pray and admit we need help. God is always present to help us in any situation, in any problem.

Marriage is what you make it. It is a sweet union, but without God in it, like all else, it is destruction waiting to happen. Be blessed in the Lord and seek Him diligently. Allow Him to be first in your life and all other things will be added unto you.

Chapter 10

Time for a Check Up!

How do you know if your marriage is in trouble? There are some basic questions that can help you determine or recognize several pertinent areas that may need specific attention before you and your mate are faced with disaster. For those special areas you both find important, write a list of them—possibly five or six—for you to discuss with each other afterward.

Directions: Answer the following questions by circling the letter that is most consistent with your point of view in a marriage relationship.

Possible answers:

D = Definitely true (10 points)

C = Undecided (1)

B = Moderately true (6 points)

A = Not at all true (3 points)

Questions:

1. Does he/she respect me as a person?

   A   B   C   D

2. Do you love it when your partner touches you throughout the day?

   A   B   C   D

3. Do you and your mate read the Bible and believe in its principles pertaining to the union of marriage? That is, equality and respect for each other?

   A   B   C   D

4. I look forward to finding time to cuddle with my partner.

   A   B   C   D

5. Does your mate do things to help you solve problems and wants to make your life nicer and easier?

   A   B   C   D

6. Do you compare your mate to someone else you may find attractive?

   A   B   C   D

7. Do you and your mate take time out of the day to affirm your love for each other by calling each other just to say "Hi" or "I love you"?

   A   B   C   D

8. I only say flattering things about my partner to others.

   A   B   C   D

9. Do you and your mate go to bed angry at each other?

    A   B   C   D

10. I love being married to my partner. I look forward to our life together.

    A   B   C   D

11. Do you find yourself resenting your partner at times?

    A   B   C   D

12. When you and your partner argue, do you go to bed angry?

    A   B   C   D

Scoring:

80–100+: **Wow!** You and your mate are totally committed totally in making your relationship work. Couples who love the Word of God and apply it to their lives are destined for success. Keep up the good work.

50–79: **Take note.** Your score is in the mid-range. It seems you are overlooking some things. Pay more attention to your relationship—it's vital to survive. It would be wise to consider using the eight steps in the chapter, *Time to Maintain a Successful Marriage,* but most of all, pray for guidance and keep God first in your lives.

0–49: **You are in trouble**. If you scored in the lowest range, you have some problems that need immediate attention, or you will find yourselves in divorce court or slipping into the *settling* stage. Don't let the enemy steal your marriage. **Fight for it.** Please consider talking to your pastor or seeking counseling from another source relevant to your situation.

Chapter 11

Time to Become One

The Conclusion

Marriage is and should be a union of beauty, respect, commitment, and love. Once we enter its sacred doors together, we are no longer separate but one. Let us continue to respect that which God has called "good" and be just that in our relationships. We were given to each other in marriage to be help mates. That means sharers of each other's burdens, hopes, aspirations, and dreams. Novelist George Elliot wrote so eloquently, "What greater thing is there for two human souls than to feel that they are joined for life—to strengthen each other in all labor, to rest on each other in all sorrow, to minister to each other in all pain, to be one with each other in silent, unspeakable memories at the moment of the last parting."

Today, if you are newlyweds or a seasoned married couple who find your marriage status slowly becoming frail, let's say this simple prayer together.

Prayer:

"Dear Father, we thank you for the union of marriage and the sanctity you have given it. We pray that you will continue to touch our marriage. Help us to be the husband and wife that you will have us to be for each other. We pray that you take the center stage in our life. Teach us patience, love, and understanding. Continue to bring us closer in our walk before you as we seek love, peace, and joy. Then and only then can our lives together reflect the love of you and display the beacon of light to those who need an example. Amen."

In closing:

Be blessed and allow yourself to love and be loved. If you will always remember the reason why you fell in love with your mate, it can be the spark to ignite your marriage fires once more. Life is only hard when we make it; marriage is one of the journeys within it. How you start your journey depends on how it will end.

Peace and blessings in your life together!

Susie

Printed in the United States
by Baker & Taylor Publisher Services